Unlocking Freedom

Connection with God

Discover your identity, heal from
the past, and find your purpose

Rachel Dick

Unlocking Freedom Workbook
Copyright © 2023 by Rachel Dick
All rights reserved.

No part of this publication may be reproduced, stored in a retrieval system or transmitted in any way or by any means, electronic, mechanical, photocopy, recording or otherwise without the prior written permission of the author except as provided by USA copyright law.

Unless otherwise indicated, all Scripture quotations are taken from the Holy Bible, New International Version, copyright © 1973, 1978, 1984, 2011 by Biblica, Inc.
Used by permission of Zondervan.
Grand Rapids, Michigan. All rights reserved.

"Breaking Soul Ties" prayer accessed through *https://app.nothinghidden.com/tools/c/0/i/9821181/soulties*.

S.H.A.P.E. Assessment accessed through Mountain Springs Church, *https://mountainsprings.org/wp-content/uploads/2016/05/SHAPE-Assessment.pdf*. Adapted from material by Rick Warren of Saddleback Church. Book adaptation, *S.H.A.P.E.: Finding and Fulfilling Your Unique Purpose for Life*, by Erik Rees.
https://static1.squarespace.com/static/599355e2bf629ad-2be88553a/t/5daa4157ba16583e195be967/1571438936679/SHAPE+assessment+new.pdf

Layout design by Kaycee Thompson
Editing by Rhonda Olson

Published in the United States of America
ISBN: 9798863994406

Unlocking Freedom

Part 1 - Connecting with God   1

    1. Knowing Who God Is   3
    2. Finding Identity in Christ   9
    3. Creating Relationship with God   15
    4. Renewing Your Mind   21
    5. Reading God's Word   27
    6. Learning to Pray   33

Part 2 - Connecting with Yourself   39

    1. Journaling the Voice of God   41
    2. Learning to Forgive   47
    3. Breaking Soul Ties   53
    4. Healing from Trauma   61
    5. Overcoming Depression & Anxiety   67
    6. Taking Care of Yourself   73

Part 3 - Connecting with Others   79

    1. Understanding God's Will   81
    2. Finding Your Purpose   87
    3. Discovering Your Gifts   91
    4. Discovering Your Place   103
    5. Exploring Further Help   117

PART ONE
CONNECTING WITH GOD

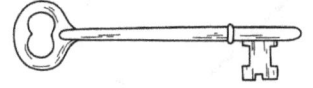

"Draw near to
God and he will
draw near to
you."
-James 4:8

SECTION ONE

KNOWING WHO GOD IS

"The Lord your God is with you, the mighty Warrior who saves. He will take great delight in you, in his love he will no longer rebuke you, but will rejoice over you with singing."
Zephaniah 3:17

PART 1 – CONNECTING WITH GOD

1 – Knowing Who God Is

God created us for communion with him. Our purpose on this earth is to love God and love people.

Matthew 22:37-40
[37] Jesus replied: "'Love the Lord your God with all your heart and with all your soul and with all your mind.' [38] This is the first and greatest commandment. [39] And the second is like it: 'Love your neighbor as yourself.' [40] All the Law and the Prophets hang on these two commandments."

If all we ever do is love God fully and love people, we've done a good job. God is a loving god. He is faithful, loyal, and caring. God is for us and not against us. He is all-knowing and all-powerful. God is our counselor and our friend. He is there for us when no one else is. You may not view God how I just described Him. If that's the case, these next few pages will help you better understand who God truly is. Before answering these questions, I want you to take a moment and invite God in. Ask God to be with you as you answer these questions and illuminate anything that needs to be brought to light. Ask Him to bring healing and restoration in the areas needed.

- o God is love – 1st John 4:7-12
- o God is always present – 1st Cor. 3:16, Psalm 139
- o God is faithful – Deut. 32:4
- o God is good – James 1:17

The scriptures above are just some of the characteristics of God. As you work through the questions below keep these scriptures in mind and see if your view of God lines up with what scripture says.

1. Typically, how you view your earthly father is how you will view your Heavenly Father. How do you view your earthly father? How did he treat you growing up? How do you view God? Do you view him as someone who will punish you if you do the wrong thing? Do you view him as a loving father who wants to lavish his love upon you? Explain.

_____

_____

_____

_____

_____

_____

2. Why do you think you view God this way? Think back to childhood. Can you tie a memory to this view? Is it the same as how you view your earthly father? If your view of God needs help, I just want to invite you right now to talk with God and tell Him you need help seeing Him as a good, loving, and faithful Father. Let him take you back to a memory when your memory of him changed. Ask him to heal that moment. Or if your view of your earthly father and God are good, journal about the goodness you see in both.

_____

_____

_____

_____

_____

_____

3. Look up the characteristics of God. Write down the ones that resonate most with you. How have you witnessed these in your life? For example: He is loving, He is faithful, He is forgiving, etc.

_____

_____

_____

_____

_____

4. Look up 3 scriptures with 3 of the characteristics you listed above. Meditate on these scriptures this week. Meditating on scriptures simply means to reread each scripture and ask yourself questions – What is this scripture saying? What does this scripture mean? What does this scripture mean for me? Constantly thinking about this scripture, just as you would when you have worrisome thoughts (over and over). Once done, come back and journal what you learned from this exercise. For example: Psalm 145:13 - He is trustworthy, Isaiah 43:1 - He is your protector, Matthew 21:22 - He is faithful.

_____

_____

_____

_____

_____

5. Do you feel like your view of God is changing? Why or why not? Are there wounds in the way that are preventing you from seeing him for who he truly is? Explain.

_____

_____

_____

_____

_____

I pray right now that you will be flooded with God's love for you. I pray you would truly see him the way that He is and that God will heal the childhood wounds of how your earthly father treated you so that you could see God as a loving God. In Jesus' name, Amen!

SECTION TWO

FINDING IDENTITY IN CHRIST

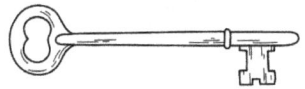

"For he has rescued us from the dominion of darkness and brought into the kingdom of the Son he loves, in whom we have redemption, the forgiveness of sins."
Colossians 1:13-14

Discovering your identity is key to fulfilling your purpose

2 – Finding Identity in Christ

Knowing who you are is one of the single most important things you can find out in life, outside of finding out who God is. If you don't know who you are, you will fall for anything. People can search for their identity all their lives in all the wrong places and never find it. This is why you see people acting differently in different crowds. For example, if a girl is dating a guy who likes rap music, but she prefers country, she may act like she likes rap music to fit in, in hopes that the guy will like her more.

I realize this is a silly example, but it can go deeper. If you don't know who you are, you are more likely to make wrong decisions to fit in, feel accepted, or gain approval. Eventually, your God-given need for love can turn into destructive behaviors. The enemy would love nothing more than to keep you bound and keep your mouth shut.

Your identity is not based on what you do, what you accomplish, or what you like. This is not a stable foundation. It is based on who God is, what he has done for you, and who you are in Him. You have to understand first what he thinks about you to understand who He is.

Look up the following scriptures. As you read them, ask yourself, "What are these scriptures saying about me?"

- Ephesians 1:4-5
- 1st John 1:9
- 1st Thess 1:4
- 1st John 4:9
- Galatians 4:7

1. What did these scriptures tell you? Did you gain a sense of who you are in Christ?

_____
_____
_____
_____
_____

2. If I was to ask you who you are, what would you say?

   _____
   _____
   _____
   _____
   _____
   _____

3. What are you passionate about? What makes you light up? What do you like to do?

   _____
   _____
   _____
   _____
   _____
   _____

4. Do you believe God loves you? Why or why not?

   _____
   _____
   _____
   _____
   _____
   _____

5. Do you believe you are forgiven? Accepted? Chosen? Why or why not?

   _____
   _____

_____
_____
_____
_____

6. List qualities and characteristics you like about yourself.

_____
_____
_____
_____
_____
_____

7. Ask someone close to you to list qualities and characteristics they see in you.

_____
_____
_____
_____
_____
_____

8. Compare the two. Did they say the same things? Did they say things you didn't? When they say things that you didn't - do you believe them? Why or why not?

_____
_____
_____
_____

9. What does God say about you? Take 5 minutes and quiet your mind. Ask God what he thinks about you and journal what you hear.

_____

_____

_____

_____

_____

Lord, I pray right now over the person doing this workbook. I pray that you would allow the blinders on their eyes to be lifted. I pray you will give them a deeper revelation of who they are and who they are in you. Help them to see you and themselves differently. In Jesus' name, Amen!

SECTION THREE

CREATING RELATIONSHIP WITH GOD

"I am the vine; you are the branches. If you remain in me and
I in you, you will bear much fruit; apart from me
you can do nothing."
John 15:5

3 – Creating Relationship with God

God created us for a relationship with Him. Our sole purpose on this earth is to be in a relationship with Him - to love God and love people.

Mark 12:30-31 "Love the Lord your God with all your heart and with all your soul and with all your mind and with all your strength.' The second is this: 'Love your neighbor as yourself.' There is no commandment greater than these."

If you never complete your long list of to-do's, just know you are loved by God regardless. If you loved Him and loved people the best you could, in the end, you will hear, "I am proud of you my good and faithful servant." We are to live our lives in such a way that it brings people to Christ. God loves us so much that he sent his only son to die for us so that we might have life.

"For God so loved the world that he gave his one and only Son, that whoever believes in him shall not perish but have eternal life." John 3:16

It doesn't matter what we have done in life, God loves us and wants to spend time with us.

What does spending time with him look like?

- Reading the Bible daily and asking him questions about what you read
- Talking with him about your day – just as you would a friend
- Praying – petitioning requests on behalf of others and for yourself
- Meditating on the Word – taking one scripture and saying it over and over. Read until you have revelation knowledge of what the scripture is saying.
- Gratitude – praising Him for who He is and what He has done
- Worshiping – playing praise & worship music
- Dancing unto the Lord
- Singing unto the Lord
- Inviting Him into your daily tasks – asking Him to be with you
- Going for a walkout in nature
- Doing something creative with Him
- Journaling His voice

He just desires to be with you, to be invited into your day, to move alongside you throughout your life. He wants a relationship with you. Think about how you would cultivate a relationship with a friend or a husband. This is exactly how we create a relationship with God. I think we get a little forgetful because He is not physically present with us, and we don't see Him right next to us. But the truth is He is right next to us always even though we cannot see Him. Do these next few exercises to start cultivating a relationship with Him.

1. Invite God into this time with Him by saying "God, I invite you into this time. Speak to me and show me that you are here with me." Ask Him to tell you what some of His favorite activities are to do with you.

   _____
   _____
   _____
   _____
   _____
   _____

2. Find a scripture that speaks to you about your current situation or your relationship with God. Write the scripture out and meditate on it – think about what it is saying and write down your thoughts. For example: If you are struggling with depression, a good scripture would be, "The joy of the Lord is my strength." Nehemiah 8:10

   _____
   _____
   _____
   _____
   _____
   _____

3. Find your favorite worship song and play it. Sit and soak in His presence. Write down anything that speaks to you through the song.

_____
_____
_____
_____
_____
_____

4. What are you grateful for? What has God done for you? What will you praise Him for all the days of your life?

_____
_____
_____
_____
_____
_____

5. Share your day with Him. Start a journal. How did your day go? What made you happy? What made you mad today? What made you sad? What do you need Him to do in your life? Who in your life needs prayer?

_____
_____
_____
_____
_____
_____

SECTION FOUR

RENEWING YOUR MIND

"Do not conform to the pattern of this world, but be
transformed by the renewing of your mind. Then you will be
able to test and approve what God's will is—his good,
pleasing and perfect will."

Romans 12:2

Renewing the mind brings Transformation

4 – Renewing Your Mind

Our minds are wired to attract our most dominant thoughts. So, it is no wonder that if you are constantly stuck thinking about how sick and tired you are, then that's the very thing you are going to create in your life – sickness and tiredness. It has been shown that trauma negatively affects the brain. So, if you have ever been through something traumatic, it's likely that your brain has gone into a survival state. This can cause depression, anxiety, or PTSD which can cause your brain to stay focused on the negative things in life.

However, it is scientifically proven we can change our brains. Our brains are neuroplastic. Meaning we can rewire them. We have the power to stop the negative loops in our brain and rewire them to be positive loops. We can rewire our brains to think and act positively, and it all starts with renewing our minds.

What does renewing your mind mean? It means literally taking the negative thoughts and replacing them with positive thoughts and feeding your mind with positive thinking.

Romans 12:2 is one of the most popular scriptures on this principle. It says, "Do not conform to the pattern of this world but be transformed by the renewing of your mind. Then you will be able to test and approve what God's will is – his good, pleasing, and perfect will."

2nd Corinthians 10:5, "We demolish arguments and every pretension that sets itself up against the knowledge of God, and we take captive every thought to make it obedient to Christ."

We replace negative thoughts with positive ones by saying, "I come out of agreement with anxiety and come into agreement with peace." You can also say, "I take authority over my thoughts, I will think on things that are good, pure, perfect, lovely, and of good report."

There are multiple ways to do this, as you will see below in the exercises, but one of the most effective ways to renew your mind is by speaking scripture over yourself. Work through the exercises below for practical application on renewing your mind.

1. Think about what you're thinking about. What are your top three thoughts that you're consumed with daily? Are they negative or positive?

   _____
   _____
   _____
   _____
   _____

2. Reframe any negative thought into a positive thought. They say for every negative thought you need to say 7 positive things. So, get in the habit of shifting the negative thoughts into positive ones. For example: I am never going to feel better. Reframe: Thank you Lord that you give me what I need each day to do the things I need to get done. Thank you for the healing that is manifesting in my body. Now, reframe some of your negative thoughts.

   _____
   _____
   _____
   _____
   _____

3. Journal your negative thoughts for the next few days. What are the negative thoughts focused on? Where do they come from? Why are they there?

   _____
   _____
   _____
   _____

4. What are your fears, insecurities, and doubts? Ask the Holy Spirit to guide you to a memory that the negative feelings/emotions are tied to. When He shows you, invite Him into that memory. Ask Him to show you where He was when it was happening. Journal below what He shows you and how it makes you feel.

5. In the same memory ask the Holy Spirit to heal your heart. Ask Him to help you forgive the person. A lot of times negative thought loops come from traumatic events. By doing these exercises this will help release you from trapped trauma and emotions in your heart, which can help you become more positive.

SECTION FIVE

READING GOD'S WORD

"Your word is a lamp to my feet and a light to my path."
Psalm 119:105

5 – Reading God's Word

Have you ever read a chapter or even a scripture in the Bible and thought, "What the heck did I just read?" Me too. Sometimes, I really struggle to understand what I am reading. Here are a few things you can do to help you with your Bible reading:

1. Make sure you are reading a version you understand well. Some easier ones to read are NLT, TPT, NIV.
2. Make sure you have a Bible where the font is easy for you to read and doesn't feel overwhelming.
3. Invite God into your Bible reading simply by saying, "God, I invite you into my reading today. I ask that you show me something new and speak to me."
4. Slow down. Even if you only read a paragraph instead of a chapter for the day. Quality over quantity. It's more important that you understand what you are reading and get something out of it than to see how much you can read.
5. If you don't understand something, go back, and read it again, until you get it.
6. If you don't understand a word – look it up.
7. Ask God questions throughout your reading.

There is an exercise called Lectio Divina. This exercise is a way to read and meditate on scripture that will help you connect with God on a personal level. It helps you know what the scripture is saying and what God is saying. This practice will help you spend time with God, create a deeper relationship with Him, and it will increase your knowledge of the Word of God. The steps to this practice are: Lectio (Read), Meditatio (Meditate), Oratio (Pray), Contemplatio (Contemplate).

Lectio (Read): Read the scripture several times. Be attentive to detail. Note verses or phrases that stand out to you. Work to understand meaning and background.

Meditatio (Meditate): Think about the reading and connect it to your life. Imagine being present to hear the passage or witness the story. Choose a word or phrase that speaks to your heart.

Oratio (Pray): Dialogue with God in prayer about the passage. Thank God for His word. Ask Him to lead you into a deeper understanding.

Contemplatio (Contemplate): Give God room to speak to you, resting in his presence, keeping an open mind and heart. Note what God is trying to teach you through the passage and time of prayer.

Let's do Lectio Divina with a few different scriptures.

- Colossians 1:4
- Ephesians 2:8-9
- 2nd Corinthians 5:17
- Philippians 4:8

Look up these scriptures and pick one that stands out to you to work through the Lectio Divina process.

1. Read – read the scripture several times. Note the details in the scriptures. What is this scripture saying? What stands out to you? What is the background of this scripture?

   _____
   _____
   _____
   _____
   _____
   _____

2. Meditate – What does this scripture mean to you? What words or phrases stand out to you?

   _____
   _____
   _____
   _____
   _____
   _____

3. Pray – Talk to God about this scripture. Ask Him to help you understand this scripture on a deeper level.

_____
_____
_____
_____
_____
_____

4. Contemplate – Ask God what He is trying to say to you through this scripture. Spend time with Him with an open heart, ready to receive from Him. Take time to journal what you hear from Him.

_____
_____
_____
_____
_____
_____

5. What are you thankful for? Spend some time in gratitude. Remember, gratitude changes the brain.

_____
_____
_____
_____
_____
_____

Now, use your own journal and do it again for another scripture of your choosing, and follow the questions above.

SECTION SIX

LEARNING TO PRAY

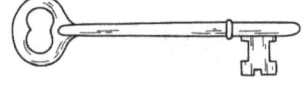

"Do not be anxious about anything, but in every situation, by prayer and supplication with thanksgiving, present your requests to God. And the peace of God, which transcends all understanding, will guard your hearts and your minds in Christ Jesus."
Phil 4:6-7

6 – Learning to Pray

When you don't know how to pray, it can be intimidating. You might be looking at how other people pray and think that you need to add in all the extra "Christianese" words like thou and thus, etc. However, praying is just a conversation with God. Just as you would talk with a friend about how your day went – God also wants to know how your day went. You can talk to him just as you would anyone else. It's creating a relationship with Him. It doesn't have to be some elaborate prayer. It can simply be, "God, I need help."

Prayer is creating a relationship through communication with God. There are different ways to pray. We have already discussed in section 5, Lectio Divina, which is praying through the Bible. There are other ways to pray as well like praying scriptures over yourself, meditating on the word, practicing God's presence, and listening. We will talk about these in the weeks to come.

Today, we are going to discuss the 5 types of prayer: supplication, thanksgiving, adoration, confession, and intercession.

Supplication means to petition or to ask for something. When you are praying you can ask God for things that line up with his will. John 14:14 says, "You may ask me for anything in my name, and I will do it." This doesn't mean that He is some genie in a bottle, and He will grant all your wishes. But He does want good for His children so ask in His name for things that you need in your life.

Thanksgiving means to be grateful for something or someone. Sing praises to him. Thank Him for all the small and big things in your life. The very fact that you have breath in your lungs is a gift from God. Find things each day to be thankful for.
Psalms 106:1 says, "Praise the Lord! Give thanks to the Lord, for he is good! His love endures forever."

Adoration means to adore, pay honor to, or gaze upon beauty. Tell God how good He is to you. Recognize God for the almighty God that He is. This would be a good place to go through the Hebrew names of God –

- o Jehovah Rapha (The Lord Who Heals You)
- o Jehovah Nissi (The Lord Is My Banner)

- Jehovah Jireh (The Lord Will Provide)
- El Elyon (The Most High God)
- Adonai (Lord, Master)
- El Shaddai (Lord God Almighty)
- Jehovah Shalom (The Lord Is Peace)

Saying these out loud brings glory to His name.

<u>Confession</u> is confessing our sins to the Father. This is the place where you tell God of all your wrongdoings and ask Him to forgive you. Once you have confessed your sin to God, He will forgive you, and your sins will be remembered no more.
1 John 1:9 says, "If we confess our sins, [God] is faithful and just and will forgive us our sins and cleanse us from all unrighteousness" (NLT)

<u>Intercession</u> is making requests to God on behalf of others. We have been given the gift of prayer, not only for ourselves but for others as well. When someone keeps coming to your mind, it is likely because God is laying them on your heart so that you can pray or intercede for them. Prayer changes things in our lives and in the lives of others. Pray and watch God work.

Prayer is life-giving communication with God and has the power to change our lives. Philippians 4:6-7 says that if we will release our worries, fears, and anxieties through prayer with supplication and thanksgiving, God will help us.

> "Do not be anxious about anything, but in every situation, by prayer and petition, with thanksgiving, present your requests to God. ⁷ And the peace of God, which transcends all understanding, will guard your hearts and your minds in Christ Jesus."

In the spaces below, pick out a few issues you have been struggling with and walk through the prayer steps with God.

1. Supplication – What are you asking God to do?

   _____

   _____

   _____

_____

_____

_____

2. Thanksgiving – What are you thankful for that He has done for you?

_____

_____

_____

_____

_____

_____

3. Adoration – Who is He to you?

_____

_____

_____

_____

_____

_____

4. Confession – What do you need forgiveness for?

_____

_____

_____

_____

_____

_____

5. Intercession – Who could use your prayers?

   _____
   _____
   _____
   _____
   _____
   _____

6. Does this way of praying help? Does it make you feel closer to God?

   _____
   _____
   _____
   _____
   _____
   _____

PART TWO

CONNECTING WITH YOURSELF

SECTION ONE

JOURNALING THE VOICE OF GOD

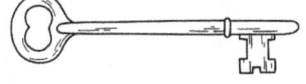

"Call to me and I will answer you, and tell you great and
unsearchable things you do not know."
Jeremiah 33:3

PART 2 – CONNECTING WITH YOURSELF

1 – Journaling the Voice of God

Journaling is something you can do for yourself that allows you to process your day. Journaling is a form of self-care. This gets all the negative out of your day. You can journal to God, to yourself, or even from God, which I will demonstrate below. I like to journal as God does special things for me or as I get words from Him so that I can look back on them during times of distress.

For the purpose of this section, we will look at journaling the voice of God. First, let's look at the types of voices you might hear when trying to hear the voice of God. Then, we will learn the steps to journal His voice.

As you grow in your relationship with God, you will start to hear from Him more and you will learn His voice. There are 3 voices we hear.

1. Our own – Our flesh will tell us all kinds of things. Our flesh wants to do things that feel good and soothe us. Our own voice can tell us it's okay to do something even when it's not because our will is so powerful and can override God's voice. Our voice might sound like – "I can do whatever I want. It won't hurt anything if I do _____. I should have the second cookie, I deserve it." We need to learn to discern our voice versus the enemy's voice.

2. The enemy's voice – The enemy is constantly trying to gain control in our minds and our souls. He can whisper things to us just like God can. It's up to us to discern the voice and either reject it or accept it. The enemy's voice can sound something like this – "You're so ugly. You will never have any friends. You should do drugs. You should isolate yourself. You will be in fear for the rest of your life." These kinds of thoughts we need to take authority over, which basically just means to reject the thought and think about something else.

    2nd Corinthians 10:5 "We take captive every thought to make it obedient to Christ."

3. God's voice – God's voice is like a whisper. It can also be a knowing or a feeling of peace or contentment. God won't speak over the chaos in our minds. So, if our thoughts are flooded with anxiety and

worry, we will have a harder time hearing his voice. God's voice might sound like this – "You are loved. You are valued. Don't do this or that because it will harm you. Talk to that person or don't talk to that person." God will never ask you to do anything that will contradict His word.

The first time I heard God's voice, I was home on a break for Christmas from a recovery program that I attended earlier in my life to get free from drug addiction (for more of the story read my book, *Finding Freedom*). I was at my brother's church, and they were having a meeting after service for a mission trip they were going on. During the meeting, I was feeling left out and sad for myself, because I couldn't go since I was going back to the recovery program. When we started to walk out of the sanctuary, I heard a small voice in my head say, "It's okay, there will be others." It felt sweet, calming, and peaceful. It was quiet yet it came with authority. I knew it wasn't my own thought, but I was still learning. I immediately turned to my brother and told him what I heard, and I asked, "Was that God?" And he said, "Sounds like it."

That was the first time I ever heard His voice. And from that moment on I started to hear from Him more and more. I tell you that story so you can get an idea for yourself of what it might sound like. God's voice will also bring comfort and peace, even when He is bringing correction or warning, there will always be peace attached to it.

Below are some steps that I learned while in Bible College that helped me learn how to hear and discern the voice of God. Follow these steps to practice.

1. Take authority over your thoughts.

    Say out loud – "I take authority over my thoughts."

2. Speak the following scriptures out loud over your mind that bring your thoughts into alignment with peace - John 10:5, 2nd Cor. 10:5, Phil 2:5-8.

    For example, you can say: "I will think on things that are good, pure, perfect, lovely and of good report." "I have the mind of Christ. I am the righteousness of God in Christ Jesus. Greater is He that is in me than He that is in the world."

3. Command all distractions to stop

   Say out loud – "I come against all distractions and hindrances. Satanic spirits – I rebuke. I plead the blood of Jesus over my mind. And I command my thoughts to line up with the Holy Spirit's thoughts and all other thoughts to flee."

4. Invite God into the space

   Say out loud – "God, I invite you into this space. I invite you to speak to me now."

5. Journal what you hear

   Now, you will journal what you hear. There are lines provided below for you to write what you hear, what you see, or what you sense. You can do this daily or weekly. The more you do it, the more you will learn to recognize what is God's voice and what isn't.

   _____
   _____
   _____
   _____
   _____
   _____
   _____
   _____
   _____
   _____
   _____
   _____
   _____
   _____
   _____

SECTION TWO

LEARNING TO FORGIVE

"And when you stand praying, if you hold anything against anyone, forgive them, so that your Father in heaven may forgive you your sins."
Mark 11:25

Forgiveness heals the heart

2 – Learning to Forgive

"Be kind and compassionate to one another, forgiving each other, just as in Christ God forgave you." – Ephesians 4:32

When someone hurts us, our initial reaction is to be offended. We typically will hold on to that offense for days, weeks, and sometimes years. We vow to ourselves that we will never trust this person or that person ever again. This eventually leads to a belief system of the world not being a safe place. We then walk around guarded. We do our best to keep people shut out of our lives, never truly letting them in.

Unforgiveness leads to bitterness and resentment in our hearts. You may think that holding on to the offense helps you in some way. In fact, you may think that not forgiving the person who hurt you is only hurting them. However, holding on to the unforgiveness only hurts you. Unforgiveness is like poison to our bodies. Holding on to unforgiveness can cause physical ailments to take root in our bodies.

Not only does releasing forgiveness over someone help you physically, but it also helps you spiritually, because when you are free from unforgiveness, then God can forgive you of your sins. Matthew 6:14 says, "For if you forgive other people when they sin against you, your heavenly Father will also forgive you." Which essentially means, that God cannot forgive you of your sins if you are holding on to an offense from someone else.

I was at a conference recently and this lady had been diagnosed with an autoimmune disease called Multiple Sclerosis (MS). MS is a disease that damages the nerves and cuts off communication from the brain to the body. MS can cause extreme pain, fatigue, depression, anxiety, and tingling in the body, among many other symptoms. She came into the conference with some kind of walking contraption that connected to her arms to help her walk. She claimed she hadn't been able to walk on her own in years. Come to find out she had some deep-seated unforgiveness towards a family member. Once the minister walked her through a prayer of forgiveness towards that person, she started walking. At first, she was walking with the help of the team, but eventually, she was walking completely on her own!

The minister then went on to say her body started breaking down due to the unforgiveness. Look at unforgiveness as black poison. It starts out as just a little bit, but it will eventually take over your whole body, brain, heart, etc.

Now, I know some of you might be saying, "But you don't know what they did to me." You're right. I don't. But it's not about what they did or didn't do to you. It's about releasing yourself from the situation. Forgiving is not saying that what the person did was okay. It's saying, "I choose to release this person and myself from the burden I have been carrying." I know this might be the hardest thing you've ever had to do, but I promise it will be worth it.

There are lines below for you to brainstorm, process, and walk through forgiving those who have hurt you. Please take your time with this. Invite God into the process. Ask Him to show you who you need to forgive. Allow Him to bring you comfort and peace.

1. Who do you need to forgive? Who has hurt you? This can be from childhood or adulthood. This can be something small or something big.

   An Indication that you have unforgiveness towards someone;
   If you think about someone who has hurt you and you still have ill feelings towards that person, that is a strong indicator that there is still unforgiveness.

   On the lines below, write out who you need to forgive.

   _____
   _____
   _____
   _____
   _____
   _____

2. What did they do to you? How did it change your life? How did it make you feel? What belief systems were created because of this event? Ex: The world is unsafe, I can't trust people, I am not worthy of love, etc.

   _____
   _____

_____

_____

_____

_____

3. Do you need to forgive yourself for anything? Have you wronged someone? Have you lived your life in a way that wasn't pleasing to God? Have you hurt family or friends? Write your thoughts on the lines below.

_____

_____

_____

_____

_____

_____

4. Walk through this prayer of forgiveness.

   Lord, I choose to forgive _____ for doing _____ to me. It hurt me very deeply, but I know that holding onto the unforgiveness is only hurting myself. I release them from the hurt they caused in my life, and I ask you to comfort me and bring me peace in this area.

   I also choose to forgive myself for any part I played in this situation. Forgive me Lord for _____. Release me from the hold that this sin has had on me and renew my heart, my mind, and my spirit.

   Help me to learn to release others immediately when they hurt me and help me to stay in a place of peace and healing.

   In Jesus' name!

5. Write out anything that came up. Did God show you anything? Did He tell you anything? Ask Him if there is anything else you need to know or see. Let Him speak to you and journal what you hear.

_____
_____
_____
_____
_____
_____
_____
_____
_____
_____
_____
_____
_____
_____
_____

SECTION THREE

BREAKING SOUL TIES

"Do you not know that he who unites himself with a prostitute is one with her in body? For it is said, "The two will become one flesh."
1st Cor 6:16

3 – Breaking Soul Ties

Soul ties are an emotional, physical, and spiritual attachment between one person and another. It is anything that ties two souls together in the spiritual realm. Soul ties can form with family members, close friends, and in intimate relationships. A person can even have a soul tie with material things. Essentially, a soul tie is anything you put above God. There are Godly soul ties and ungodly soul ties.

GODLY SOUL TIES

Godly soul ties are explained in the Bible in Mark 10:8, "and the two will become one flesh. So, they are no longer two but one flesh." Soul ties in marriage are Godly soul ties and tie a husband and wife together spiritually. This kind of soul tie was intended to be unbreakable by man. This is why you feel magnetized to your mate.

In the Bible, Jonathan & David had a very close friendship, and a Godly soul tie formed. 1st Samuel 18:1 describes their relationship, "As soon as he had finished speaking to Saul, the soul of Jonathan was knit to the soul of David, and Jonathan loved him as his own soul." (ESV) This shows that soul ties can be formed not only through sexual relationships but also through close friendships and family.

UNGODLY SOUL TIES

Ungodly soul ties are ties that have been formed that God never intended to happen. This can be through sex outside of marriage or through relationships that are toxic. 1st Corinthians 6:16 (ESV) says, "Or don't you know that he who unites himself with a prostitute is one with her in body? For it is said, "…the two will become one flesh." Genesis 2:24 (ESV). This again proves the Biblical truth of soul ties.

Ever wonder why women continue to keep going back to men who hurt them? Or maybe this is you... Maybe your husband or boyfriend continues to beat you and you feel a need to stay with him. This is due to soul ties. Inside of marriage soul ties strengthen your relationships. They keep you connected on a deep physical and spiritual level. Outside of marriage, they can be damaging.

Soul ties can be formed with anything you put in the place of God. If you are going consistently to someone for advice before asking God, an ungodly soul tie can form. Soul ties naturally form in child/parent relationships. If the relationship is toxic, an ungodly soul tie can form. This can even happen with drugs. If someone is addicted to drugs an ungodly soul tie can be formed with drugs due to the person putting substances above God.

WAYS A SOUL TIE CAN FORM

- Soul ties can be formed when we are trying to fill a void in our hearts that only God can fill.
- If you are living together with someone and you break up.
- If you divorce someone.
- Close relationships – good or bad.
- Anything you put above God.

I like to use this illustration:

Envision a paper heart - Let's say in elementary school you really liked this boy, and you gave him a piece of your heart (tear a piece of the paper heart off) and eventually he hurt your heart. Then in middle school, it happened again (tear a piece of the heart off), and in high school, you found the one you were going to marry only for him to break your heart (tear a piece of the heart off). Eventually, you get married only for it to end in divorce (tear another piece of the heart off). As you can see you will be left with a mangled heart with barely any pieces left. This is what happens when your heart is unhealed.

In the Bible, they didn't always have rabbis around to perform marriages. If you slept with someone, you were considered married. A sign of marriage was that a person had sexual intercourse with another person. Once a couple had sex, they formed a new covenant between themselves and their spouse. This would separate them from their families. Just like in Mark 10:8 – the two become one. This means that all their spiritual baggage becomes yours. If they struggle with anger, you could now start struggling with anger and not realize why. Same thing with addictions, depression, anxiety, etc. I was talking to a recently married couple, and they were telling me that each of them started struggling with things that their partner had previously struggled with once they consecrated their marriage. You take on everything from your partner when you choose to have sex with them. Baggage and all.

Another illustration I like to use that paints a perfect picture of a soul tie is to think about gluing two different colored pieces of paper together. For this example, let's say one piece of paper is blue and one is pink. Once the glue is dry – try pulling the two pieces of paper away from each other. What you will find is the two pieces of paper will not come apart easily nor will they come apart still intact. You will see blue pieces on the pink and pink pieces on the blue. Both pieces of paper are no longer whole pieces of paper. They are both broken and in need of repair/healing. This is what happens when we have created ungodly soul ties and try to leave the situation without healing. We are unhealed with wounded hearts. In this instance, if we were to try and step into another relationship or another marriage, we would be giving someone a heart that is not whole, and we wouldn't be able to fully love them in the same capacity as if we had a healed heart.

It's important to heal your heart fully before stepping into another relationship.

SIGNS YOU HAVE AN UNGODLY SOUL TIE

- It feels like a part of you has left
- You have a longing for people you have slept with
- Feeling emotionally or physically attached to someone who continues to hurt you
- Defending that person regardless of what others say
- Still obsessively thinking about an ex-years later
- Taking on traits of those you have slept with such as their addictions, sicknesses, unhealthy thought patterns, etc.
- Being manipulated or controlled

Here's the good news – you can break soul ties. You can fully and completely heal your heart so that you can stop being tormented by the past. Follow through with the steps below to experience freedom and healing in this area of your life.

1. Sit down and ask the Holy Spirit to show you who and what you need to break soul ties with. Take your time on this so that you can make sure you get your heart fully healed. Use the lines below to write down what you hear.

_____

_____

_____

_____

_____

_____

2. Once you have the list of people and things you need to break soul ties with, ask the Holy Spirit to help you through this process. It might bring up old feelings and potentially could make you sad. Ask the Holy Spirit to comfort you and to help you fully break these ties that have had you bound for years.

3. Below you will find a prayer to pray. Work through the prayer one at a time putting in the blanks the name of each person and thing you wrote down in step #1.

4. In the name of Jesus, I break the power of all ungodly spirit, soul, and bodily ties created between _____ and me.

   By the power of the cross, I send back to _____ all parts of him/her/it that they gave to me that never belonged to me.

   And I take back from _____ all parts of me that I gave to them that never belonged to them.

   Father, I ask you to set a guard over my spirit, soul, and body to never again connect with _____ in this ungodly way.

   I nail to the cross the lie that joining with _____ in any of these ungodly ways was necessary, needed, or wanted on my part.

   I break all agreements I've made with this lie, known or unknown, and I turn away from joining with it.

   Father, as you send this lie away from me, what is the truth about this situation you want me to know?

   Journal below what you hear from God.

   _____

   _____

SECTION FOUR

HEALING FROM TRAUMA

"He heals the brokenhearted and binds up their wounds."
Psalm 147:3

Don't let pain turn your heart into something UGLY

4 – Healing from Trauma

According to American Psychological Association, "trauma is defined as an emotional response to a terrible event like an accident, rape, or natural disaster." Trauma can cause a person to not be able to cope after the accident. It leads to shock and denial. Left undealt with, it can and will eventually lead to physical symptoms manifesting in the body because of the lasting emotional response from the undealt with trauma. Experiencing trauma can harm a person's sense of self and ability to regulate emotions and navigate relationships.

Adverse Childhood Experiences, also known as ACEs, are traumatic events that occur during childhood. The concept of ACEs originated in a study in 1995 by the Centers for Disease Control & the Kaiser Permanente Health Care Organization. In this study, they found that there were two forms of abuse a person could go through in life - something happening to them personally and/or something happening to their family. The study discovered that the more ACEs you have in childhood, the more likely you are to experience the same things in adulthood.

Here is the list. As you read them, count how many you have experienced.

Personal:

1. Physical abuse
2. Verbal abuse
3. Sexual abuse
4. Physical neglect
5. Emotional neglect

Related to other family members:

1. A parent who was addicted to drugs or alcohol
2. A parent who was a victim of domestic violence
3. A family member who went to jail
4. A family member who was diagnosed with a mental illness
5. Experiencing the divorce of parents

It is said if you have 2 or more of these experiences, then you had a traumatic childhood. If you have experienced any of the ACEs, you are more likely to do drugs, become obese, be easily overwhelmed by stress, have chronic illness, have depression and anxiety, struggle with suicide, and be diagnosed with many different diseases and potentially cancers.

Going through traumatic events causes emotional dysregulation which can lead to being stuck in a state of fight, flight (hypervigilance), or freeze. As previously stated, undealt with trauma leads to physical symptoms in the body, such as: anxiety, depression, stress, stomach problems, pain, chronic fatigue, etc.

So, that's all the bad news! I don't give you all this information so that you can get upset and stay stuck in the "poor me" mentality. I share this information because knowledge brings revelation which in turn brings transformation.

Now, here is the good news! Trauma can be healed with God. Our brains are plastic or malleable. They have the ability to rewire themselves and change. We even see multiple scriptures that tell us to be transformed by the renewing of your mind (Romans 12:2) and that if we take our thoughts captive (2nd Cor. 2:5) and pull down strongholds (2nd Cor. 10:4), that we have the power to change our brain!

Throughout the Bible, we see many who went through traumatic events. Noah saw the entire world destroyed. Joseph was sold into slavery and betrayed by his family. Daniel almost died in the lion's den. Job lost everything. Paul was beaten and put into prison multiple times. However, one thing all of these people had in common was they had God. They never lost their faith. They chose to cling to God through all of the hardships, regardless of their circumstances, and God redeemed them.

We are reminded in Deuteronomy 31:6 that God is always with us. "Be strong and courageous. Do not be afraid or terrified because of them, for the Lord your God goes with you; he will never leave you nor forsake you." And again, in Isaiah 41:10 (NLT), "Don't be afraid, for I am with you. Don't be discouraged, for I am your God. I will strengthen you and help you. I will hold you up with my victorious right hand."

The exercises below will help you reframe the trauma and rewire your brain to heal the parts of your brain that have been traumatized and stuck. Work through these questions thoughtfully and prayerfully. The amount of effort you put into this process will determine how much you get out of it.

1. We run around this world believing lies that simply are not true. Things happen to us in childhood that cause us to question truths

we have been believing and sometimes they turn into wrong belief systems. Ask God to reveal any lies that you have been believing. Ex: No one could ever love me; I am alone in this world; I am not good enough; People don't like me, etc. Write them down as you hear them and think of them.

_____

_____

_____

_____

_____

2. Now, replace the lie with the truth. Think of what the opposite of the lie is. For instance, the lie might be "I will always be depressed." The opposite of depression is joy. So, the truth could be "The joy of the Lord is my strength." Take some time to write out the truths to replace the lies. Once you have done that, speak these out loud daily. For example: "I come out of agreement with the lie that I am worthless, and I come into agreement with the truth that I am chosen by God to do His good works." You might put these on notecards and put them around your house or write them with a dry-erase marker on your mirror. Confessing these truths over your life daily will help solidify it in your heart.

_____

_____

_____

_____

_____

3. Another useful tool is something I like to call Reframing Memories. If you have bad memories that pop up and haunt you periodically, this is a great tool to help take the sting out of the memory. Each time a memory comes up, look at it as an opportunity to heal. In-

stead of trying to push it down and not deal with it, take it to God, and walk through the healing process. As the memories come up, follow the steps below.

- Invite God into the memory
- Ask Him where He was in that specific memory
- Ask Him to heal your heart in that moment
- Ask Him if you need to forgive anyone
- Then release that memory to Him to heal

I have done this in my own life – A LOT – and it has been healing.

It is God's will for you to prosper and be in good health even as your soul prospers. 3rd John 1:2 (NKJV)

Use the lines below to journal anything that comes up.

_____

_____

_____

_____

_____

_____

_____

_____

_____

_____

_____

_____

SECTION FIVE

OVERCOMING DEPRESSION & ANXIETY

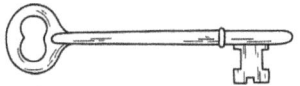

"Peace I leave with you; my peace I give you. I do not give to you as the world gives. Do not let your hearts be troubled and do not be afraid."

John 14:27

Let your heart be filled with peace

5 – Overcoming Depression and Anxiety

More than 1 in 5 adults live with a mental illness. It is said that at least half of the population will struggle with a mental health condition at least some point in their life even if only temporarily. Depression and anxiety can be crippling, and they can feel like there is no hope or no help.

Philippians 4:6-7 says, "Do not be anxious about anything, but in everything by prayer and supplication with thanksgiving let your requests be made known to God. And the peace of God, which surpasses all understanding, will guard your hearts and your minds in Christ Jesus."

And Matthew 11:28 says, "Come to me, all you who are weary and burdened, and I will give you rest."

And Psalm 34:18 says, "The Lord is near to the brokenhearted and saves the crushed in spirit."

I could go on. The Bible is full of scriptures to bring comfort and encouragement to those struggling with depression. It has many scriptures that instruct us on what to do with anxiety. However, what do we do when we are following the instructions of the Bible, reading the Word, and spending time with God and nothing seems to be working?

Well-meaning people used to tell me I needed to pray more, believe more, read my Bible more, etc. Although those are great things to do, sometimes that just isn't enough. I'm not saying that God can't perform miraculous healings, because He most certainly can. I've experienced it. However, sometimes that's just not the case, and we have to walk it out. So, what do we do in these times?

It's important when trying to overcome mental health challenges that you focus on the whole person. Don't just focus on the brain. Focus on the body and spirit, too. Below is a list of strategies that when done together with other things will help boost your mental health.

1. Keep a gratitude journal. It is scientifically proven that anxiety and gratitude cannot take up space in the brain at the same time. Write out 5 things you are grateful for every single day.
2. Keep a journal where you can process your emotions daily.
3. Talk with a friend or mentor to help you see that you are not alone. Support is key.

4. Go for a walk. Getting out in nature is medicine and can shift your focus.
5. Sit in the sun. Sun is medicine and can boost your vitamin D levels.
6. Check for vitamin deficiencies.
7. Make sure you are drinking enough water daily.
8. Get some exercise. Move your body daily.
9. Stop negative thoughts and exchange them with positive ones.
10. Make sure you aren't eating a bunch of processed foods.
11. Reduce your sugar and caffeine intake.
12. Get a SAD lamp for seasonal depression due to less exposure to sunlight.
13. Diffuse oils. Oils that can help with mental health include: Joy, Lavender, Cedarwood, Bergamot, White Angelica, Peace and calming, Valor, Ylang Ylang, Frankincense, Lemon, and Peppermint.
14. Do deep breathing exercises. Breathe in for a count of 4, hold for 4, breathe out for 4, hold for 4. This will calm down cortisol levels.
15. Stop being so hard on yourself. Think about how far you have come and celebrate your progress.
16. Get up, get out of bed, and get ready anyway – this can do wonders for your mood.
17. Create routines and structure.
18. Listen to music.
19. Dance.
20. Shake it out. Get up and shake your whole body. This can get you out of your feelings and regulate your nervous system.
21. YouTube videos on tapping.
22. Do something creative.
23. Volunteer somewhere. This will get your perspective off of yourself and onto others.
24. Meditate on the goodness of God, and all that He has done for you. (See section 1 in Part 1 for reference on meditation.)
25. Get at least 7-8 hours of sleep at night.
26. Seek therapy if needed.
27. Remind yourself that God is with you and that you are never alone.
28. Reach out to someone whom you feel comfortable with to ask for help if needed!

This list could go on and on. There are many things you can do in conjunction with believing God for a miracle and trusting that He will help you through the tough times.

Below is an exercise you can do with any event that triggers any kind of negative emotions you don't want. It's called Chasing the Trigger. When something triggers you and causes anxiety, depression, anger, etc. ask yourself these questions:

1. What was the event that triggered me?

   _____
   _____
   _____
   _____
   _____
   _____

2. What feelings did it cause?

   _____
   _____
   _____
   _____
   _____
   _____

3. When was the first time in your life that you felt this way? (Dig back into your past. Ask God to show you if nothing is coming to mind.)

   _____
   _____
   _____
   _____
   _____
   _____

4. What was the lie you chose to believe from that situation? When we go through negative experiences, we tend to create negative belief systems or lies. For example: I will always be rejected, I will always be fearful, I will never be worthy of love. Figure out what lies you have been believing from the original memory.

_____
_____
_____
_____
_____
_____

5. What is the truth about the situation? Now come up with the opposite of the lie. For example: I am loved, I am worthy of having friends, I am accepted, etc.

_____
_____
_____
_____
_____
_____

Once you've gone through and answered all the questions, take it all to God. Ask Him to heal you from the original memory where the lies were formed, and negative belief systems started. Come out of agreement with the lie and into agreement with the truth.

We touched on this in the trauma section. If you need a prayer to follow, you can go back to section 4 and follow the same pattern.

This is something you can do on a daily basis as moments in life trigger you, you can stop and run through this list of questions and start healing from the original memories that caused the lies and negative belief systems.

SECTION SIX

TAKING CARE OF YOURSELF

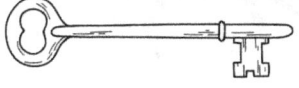

"...And he said to them, "Come with me by yourselves to a quiet place and get some rest."
Mark 6:31

6 – Taking Care of Yourself

Some people mistake self-care for selfishness. In fact, this couldn't be further from the truth. If you are severely depressed and dealing with pain from your past, you likely won't be able to effectively help someone else. Self-care is important because it sets you up to be energized, healed, and whole in order to bring healing to others. Without taking care of yourself, you could find yourself in a dark place, experiencing burnout, and needing to take time off of work to feel a sense of normalcy. If we are intentional about taking care of ourselves, then we can live a fuller, happier, healthier life.

Biblical self-care is stewarding everything God gives you – your body, mind, spirit, health, finances, relationships, belongings, etc. This means spending time with God, eating healthy, working out, reading our Bible, changing limiting belief systems, going to counseling, doing things that promote growth, and doing things that bring joy, happiness, and peace.

Taking care of yourself is just as important as taking care of others. If you don't take care of yourself first, then you will be too depleted to take care of anyone else. Just as they say on an airplane, put on your mask first if the plane is going down before you try to help someone else. You must do the same in real life.

In Proverbs 4:23, it says, "Above all else, guard your heart, for everything you do flows from it." This means taking care of ourselves. Above all else, we must guard and take care of our hearts. God thought our hearts were so important that He told us to guard them above everything else.

When we are taking care of others and not taking care of ourselves, we can experience burnout. This is not honoring our hearts or our bodies. It's important that we find things that bring us joy and fulfillment outside of taking care of others in order to honor ourselves and God.

In Luke 10:27, it says, "…love your neighbor as yourself." This implies that we must first love and care for ourselves before we are able to love and care for others well.

What does taking care of ourselves look like?

It looks like finding things to do that bring us joy, peace, love, and simply make us feel better. Included in this would be rest. If you are one of those people who just go go go and never stop to rest – you could potentially experience burnout soon. It is important that we take periods of time throughout our weeks to rest and re-energize. In Mark 6:30-45, Jesus Himself told them to come with Him to a quiet place to get some rest. Sometimes we just need to shut the world out for a couple of hours and focus on ourselves and our peace.

Below is a list of things that are considered self-care activities. Figure out what works best for you and start implementing a few things each week.

1. Eat healthy
2. Work out
3. Go for walks in nature
4. Process emotions
5. Journal your day
6. Light a candle
7. Drink a cup of tea or coffee
8. Watch a funny movie
9. Spend time with a close friend
10. Take a Zumba class
11. Journal the voice of God
12. Take a dance class
13. Do something artsy
14. Practice mindfulness
15. Get a massage
16. Play your favorite songs
17. Take a break from social media
18. Get your nails done
19. Go shopping
20. Take a bath
21. Do some gardening
22. Do some stretching
23. Diffuse some oils

The list could go on and on. Find out what works best for you and implement those things into your daily/weekly life.

1. What are your thoughts on self-care? Do you believe it's selfish or Biblical? Explain.

   _____
   _____
   _____
   _____
   _____
   _____

2. Do you take care of yourself well? Why or why not?

   _____
   _____
   _____
   _____
   _____
   _____

3. What could you do better?

   _____
   _____
   _____
   _____
   _____
   _____

4. What are some self-care activities you could add to your daily life? What about weekly?

   _____
   _____

_____

_____

_____

_____

5. Do a couple of the listed activities above. Monitor how you feel before the activity, during, and after. Journal below how the activities made you feel.

_____

_____

_____

_____

_____

_____

PART THREE
CONNECTING WITH OTHERS

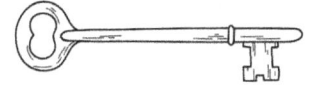

"My command is this: Love each other as I have loved you."
—John 15:12

SECTION ONE
UNDERSTANDING GOD'S WILL

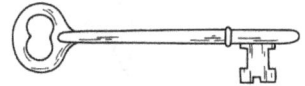

"I delight to do Your will, my God; Your Law is within my heart."
Psalms 40:8

PART 3 – CONNECTING WITH OTHERS

1 – Understanding God's Will

Now that you have learned how to connect with God and connect with yourself, it is time to learn how to connect with others. In Mark 12:30-31 it says, "You must love the Lord your God with all your heart, all your soul, all your mind, and all your strength. The second is equally important: Love your neighbor as yourself. No other commandment is greater than these."

Having a relationship with Christ comes first. Then, from the overflow of the relationship with Him, you should not only love others but love them well. The two most important things on this earth are to love God by spending time with Him, creating a relationship with Him, and loving others and leading them to Christ.

According to Mark 16:15, we are called to go into all the world and proclaim the gospel. This means living your life in such a way that honors God and points people to God. People should be able to look at you and see that you're different. People should feel God's love through you. We should make it our mission to bring those to Christ who don't know Him.

For some, this may look like loving on your next-door neighbor by doing special things for them. For another, this may look like preaching from a pulpit. This could be as simple as making a meal for someone or smiling at someone in the store. I think sometimes we think if we aren't actively out on the street evangelizing people then we aren't doing good enough or aren't fulfilling God's purpose on this earth. I used to get caught up in this thinking. However, when God presses upon your heart to pray for someone, it doesn't always have to be an outward action in public. It can be an intercession within yourself for that person. It's important to ask God what He wants you to do when He lays someone on your heart, and then be obedient to what He says.

We are ambassadors of Christ on this earth. 2nd Corinthians 5:20 says, "So we are Christ's ambassadors; God is making his appeal through us. We speak for Christ when we plead, 'Come back to God!'" Being ambassadors means being sensitive to the Holy Spirit. When He says speak, we speak. When He says move, we move. Just simply loving on people, praying for them, and leading them towards God.

1. What kind of experience do you have with helping or caring for people? Is this hard for you?

   _____

   _____

   _____

   _____

   _____

   _____

2. How do you think an ambassador of Christ should live their life?

   _____

   _____

   _____

   _____

   _____

   _____

3. Do you feel like you represent God well? Why or why not?

   _____

   _____

   _____

   _____

   _____

   _____

4. Do you love other people well? What is an area you could start to work on?

_____
_____
_____
_____
_____

5. Think of one person that you could do something for – either praying, making a meal, having a conversation, etc. After you do the activity, journal about your experience. Did it make you feel good about yourself? How did the other person respond?

_____
_____
_____
_____
_____

6. Does having conversations about God with non-believers make you feel anxious? If so, why do you think that is?

_____
_____
_____
_____
_____

SECTION TWO

FINDING YOUR PURPOSE

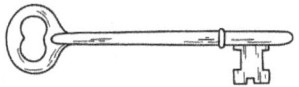

"For I know the plans I have for you," declares the Lord, "plans to prosper you and not to harm you, plans to give you hope and a future."

Jeremiah 29:11

2 – Finding Your Purpose

Many walk around this world lost and searching for a purpose. The dictionary defines purpose as the reason for which something exists or a goal to be obtained. Many people think we are here on this earth for ourselves aimlessly wandering around doing whatever we please to bring ourselves pleasure. However, there are countless scriptures saying we are here to love others and help them find Christ.

- **John 15:12** - "…love each other as I have loved you."
- **Phil 2:4** - "Not looking to your own interests but each of you to the interests of the others."
- **Hebrews 13:16** - "And do not forget to do good and to share with others, for with such sacrifices God is pleased."
- **Matthew 10:8** - "Heal the sick, raise the dead, cleanse those who have leprosy, drive out demons. Freely you have received; freely give."

Our purpose on this earth is to love God and love people. This may look different for each person. Some have hearts for single moms, or orphaned children, while others have hearts for the homeless or drug addicts. It's important to find out what people group you feel called to and to find out what your giftings are for you to walk in your purpose.

Everyone is given different giftings by God for others. 1st Corinthians 12:7-11 mentions 9 different gifts that anyone can flow in and out of. Typically, people will be more gifted in certain areas. However, anyone at any time can flow in and out of any of these giftings.

1. Word of wisdom – having insight into someone's future.
2. Word of knowledge – having insight into someone's past.
3. Faith – having the ability to believe in big things.
4. Gifts of healing – being able to lay hands on people and see them be healed.
5. Miracles – having the faith and ability to pray for things and see miracles happen.
6. Prophecy – words from God for the body of Christ that equips people through exhortation, edification, and encouragement.
7. Discernment of spirits – being able to tell what kind of spirit is operating in a certain situation or person.
8. Tongues – speaking in an unknown language from the Holy Spirit to give a message to a congregation.
9. Interpretation of tongues – when a public word is given in tongues

there must be an interpretation that comes from the Holy Spirit through a person.

There are more gifts mentioned in Ephesians 4:11-13 & 1st Corinthians 12:27-30. Some of these gifts are known as the 5-fold ministry gifts. These are God-given gifts that people contribute to congregations and ministries.

1. Apostle – a person who can influence and lead and is sent out to spread the gospel.
2. Prophet – a person who speaks for God by divine inspiration.
3. Evangelist – a person who preaches God's Word publicly to crowds to save souls.
4. Pastor – a minister in charge of a congregation who teaches and preaches the Word.
5. Teacher – a person who has a preaching and teaching ministry who communicates biblical truth for transformation.

There are other gifts listed throughout the Bible and in the next couple of sections, you will have a chance to explore those in more depth and find out what giftings you hold within you. Remember these giftings are for others. 1 Peter 4:10 says, "God has given each of you a gift from his great variety of spiritual gifts. Use them well to serve one another." (NLT)

We are called to be the salt and light of the earth. Matthew 5:14-16 depicts this well. It says, "You are the light of the world. A town built on a hill cannot be hidden. Neither do people light a lamp and put it under a bowl. Instead, they put it on its stand, and it gives light to everyone in the house. In the same way, let your light shine before others, that they may see your good deeds and glorify your Father in heaven." This means we are to lead by example, love others well, and point them to Christ. Finding your place will help you feel fulfilled and will give you a sense of purpose.

This should be an exciting and fun time of discovery. Before you begin the next section, invite God into this time. Ask Him to help you answer the questions accurately and to bring to remembrance all things needed. Don't overthink anything. Answer how you truly are and not how you want to be to get the most accurate results. When you're ready, head on over to the next section!

SECTION THREE

DISCOVERING YOUR GIFTS

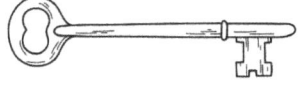

"Each of you should use whatever gift you have received to serve others, as faithful stewards of God's grace in its various forms."
1st Peter 4:10

You are Important
Your presence matters

3 - Discovering Your Gifts

S.H.A.P.E.

The S.H.A.P.E. assessment was developed by Rick Warren and Saddleback church. It is designed to help you better understand your gifts, your passions, and how you can serve in your church. The assessment has five sections that are meant to capture a holistic view of your unique abilities:

- **Spiritual Gifts Inventory:** The first section of the assessment will help you determine what gifts God has given to you.

- **Heart / Passion Assessment:** Next, you will consider what you are passionate about.

- **Abilities Assessment:** In this section, you will list the special skills and abilities you possess.

- **Personality Assessment:** You will gain insight into your personality and motivations.

- **Experiences:** In this last section, you will describe the experiences that have shaped you, whether those are spiritual, educational, or professional experiences.

This summary of your gifts, passions, skills, personality, and experiences will help you uncover and develop your areas of ministry both inside and outside of the church. The goal of this assessment is to give you direction, affirm what you already know, and provide guidance.

Five Ways God Has **Shaped** You for Service

S	Spiritual Gifts	What has God supernaturally gifted me to do?
H	Heart	What do I have a passion for and love to do?
A	Abilities	What natural talents and skills do I have?
P	Personality	Where does my personality best suit me to serve?
E	Experiences	What spiritual experiences have I had?

Spiritual Gifts Assessment

"Now about spiritual gifts, brothers, I do not want you to be ignorant."
1 Corinthians 12:1

A spiritual gift is a special ability given by the Holy Spirit to serve others and strengthen the Body of Christ.

Ways to Discover Our Spiritual Gifts:

- Experiment – It's easier to discover your gift through ministry than to discover your ministry through your gift.
- Read and study – There are several books that talk about spiritual gifts.
- Take assessments – Such as the S.H.A.P.E. assessment.
- Ask others for input – Others will often see gifts in us that we can't see ourselves.

Spiritual Gifts Assessment:

Directions: Respond to each statement on the Spiritual Gift Assessment pages which follow according to the following scale:

3 = Consistently, definitely true

2 = Most of the time, usually true

1 = Some of the time, once in a while

0 = Not at all, never

Use the answer key to write your responses to each statement in the box that corresponds to that statement.

Important: Answer according to who you are, not who you would like to be or think you ought to be. How true are these statements for you? What has been your experience? To what degree do these statements reflect your usual tendencies?

Total each row and record that number in the Total (T) column on page 102. Example:

| 1= 3 | 18= 2 | 35= 3 | 52= 1 | 69= 2 | 86= 3 | 103= 1 | T= 15 | A |

When you have completed the assessment, please transfer your **top three to five Spiritual Gifts** to your S.H.A.P.E. Profile. (The top 3-6 highest totals (T's) = corresponding letters to be transferred into the profile). Use the separate answer key and put the top 3 to 6 Spiritual Gifts on page 115.

_____ 1. I like to organize people, tasks, and events.
_____ 2. I would like to start churches in places where they do not presently exist.
_____ 3. I enjoy working creatively with wood, cloth, paints, metal, glass, or other materials.
_____ 4. I enjoy challenging people's perspectives of God by using various forms of art.
_____ 5. I can readily distinguish between spiritual truth and error, good and evil.
_____ 6. I tend to see the potential in people.
_____ 7. I communicate the gospel to others with clarity and effectiveness.
_____ 8. I find it natural and easy to trust God to answer my prayers.
_____ 9. I give liberally and joyfully to people in financial need or to projects requiring support.
_____ 10. I enjoy working behind the scenes to support the work of others.
_____ 11. I view my home as a place to minister to people in need.
_____ 12. I take prayer requests from others and consistently pray for them.
_____ 13. I am approached by people who want to know my perspective on a particular passage or biblical truth.
_____ 14. I can motivate others to accomplish a goal.
_____ 15. I empathize with hurting people and desire to help in their healing process.
_____ 16. I can speak in a way that results in conviction and change in the lives of others.
_____ 17. I enjoy spending time nurturing and caring for others.
_____ 18. I can communicate God's work effectively.

---

3 = Consistently, 2 = Most of the time, 1 = Some of the time, 0 = Not at all

_____ 19. I am often sought out by others for advice about spiritual or personal matters.
_____ 20. I am careful, thorough, and skilled at managing details.
_____ 21. I am attracted to the idea of serving in another country or ethnic community.
_____ 22. I am skilled in working with different kinds of tools.
_____ 23. I enjoy developing and using my artistic skills (art, drama, music, photography, etc.).
_____ 24. I frequently can judge a person's character based on first impressions.
_____ 25. I enjoy reassuring and strengthening those who are discouraged.
_____ 26. I consistently look for opportunities to build relationships with non-Christians.
_____ 27. I have confidence in God's continuing provision and help, even in difficult times.
_____ 28. I give more than a tithe so that kingdom work can be accomplished.
_____ 29. I enjoy doing routine tasks that support the ministry.
_____ 30. I enjoy meeting new people and helping them to feel welcome.
_____ 31. I enjoy praying for long periods of time and receive leadings as to what God wants me to pray for.
_____ 32. I receive information from the Spirit that I did not acquire through natural means.
_____ 33. I can influence others to achieve a vision.
_____ 34. I can patiently support those going through painful experiences as they try to stabilize their lives.
_____ 35. I feel responsible for confronting others with the truth.
_____ 36. I have compassion for wandering believers and want to protect them.
_____ 37. I can spend time studying knowing that presenting the truth will make a difference in the lives of people.
_____ 38. I can often find simple, practical solutions in the midst of conflict or confusion.

---

3 = Consistently, 2 = Most of the time, 1 = Some of the time, 0 = Not at all

_____ 39. I can clarify goals and develop strategies or plans to accomplish them.
_____ 40. I am willing to take an active part in starting a new church.
_____ 41. I enjoy making things for use in ministry.
_____ 42. I help people understand themselves, their relationships, and God better through artistic expression.
_____ 43. I can see through phoniness or deceit before it is evident to others.
_____ 44. I give hope to others by directing them to the promises of God.
_____ 45. I am effective at adapting the gospel message so that it connects with an individual's felt needs.
_____ 46. I believe that God will help me to accomplish great things.
_____ 47. I manage my money well in order to free more of it for giving.
_____ 48. I willingly take on a variety of odd jobs around the church to meet the needs of others.
_____ 49. I genuinely believe the Lord directs strangers to me who need to get connected to others.
_____ 50. I am conscious of ministering to others as I pray.
_____ 51. I am committed, and schedule blocks of time for reading and studying Scripture, to understand Biblical truthfully and accurately.
_____ 52. I can adjust my leadership style to bring out the best in others.
_____ 53. I enjoy helping people sometimes regarded as undeserving or beyond help.
_____ 54. I boldly expose cultural trends, teachings, or events, that contradict Biblical principles.
_____ 55. I like to provide guidance for the whole person – relationally, emotionally, spiritually, etc.
_____ 56. I can devote considerable time to learning new Biblical truths in order to communicate them to others.
_____ 57. I can easily select the most effective course of action from among several alternatives.
_____ 58. I can identify and effectively use the resources needed to accomplish tasks.

---

3 = Consistently, 2 = Most of the time, 1 = Some of the time, 0 = Not at all

_____ 59. I can adapt well to different cultures and surroundings.
_____ 60. I can visualize how something should be constructed before I build it.
_____ 61. I like finding new and fresh ways of communicating God's truth.
_____ 62. I tend to see rightness or wrongness in situations.
_____ 63. I reassure those who need to take courageous action in their faith, family, or life.
_____ 64. I invite unbelievers to accept Christ as their Savior.
_____ 65. I trust God in circumstances where success cannot be guaranteed by human effort alone.
_____ 66. I am challenged to limit my lifestyle in order to give away higher percentages of my income.
_____ 67. I see spiritual significance in doing practical tasks.
_____ 68. I like to create a place where people do not feel that they are alone.
_____ 69. I pray with confidence because I know that God works in response to prayer.
_____ 70. I have insight or just know something to be true.
_____ 71. I set goals and manage people and resources effectively to accomplish them.
_____ 72. I have great compassion for hurting people.
_____ 73. I see most actions as right or wrong and feel the need to correct the wrong.
_____ 74. I can faithfully provide long-term support and concern for others.
_____ 75. I like to take a systematic approach to my study of the Bible.
_____ 76. I can anticipate the likely consequences of an individual's or a group's action.
_____ 77. I like to help organizations or groups become more efficient.
_____ 78. I can relate to others in culturally sensitive ways.
_____ 79. I honor God with my handcrafted gifts.
_____ 80. I apply various artistic expressions to communicate God's truth.
_____ 81. I receive affirmation from others concerning the reliability of my insights or perceptions.

---

3 = Consistently, 2 = Most of the time, 1 = Some of the time, 0 = Not at all

_____ 82. I strengthen those who are wavering in their faith.
_____ 83. I openly tell people that I am a Christian and want them to ask me about my faith.
_____ 84. I am convinced of God's daily presence and action in my life.
_____ 85. I like knowing that my financial support makes a real difference in the lives and ministries of God's people.
_____ 86. I like to find small things that need to be done and often do them without being asked.
_____ 87. I enjoy entertaining people and opening my home to others.
_____ 88. When I hear about needy situations, I feel burdened to pray.
_____ 89. I have suddenly known some things about others but did not know how I knew them.
_____ 90. I influence others to perform to the best of their capability.
_____ 91. I can look beyond a person's handicaps or problems to see a life that matters to God.
_____ 92. I like people who are honest and will speak the truth.
_____ 93. I enjoy giving guidance and practical support to a small group of people.
_____ 94. I can communicate Scripture in ways that motivate others to study and want to learn more.
_____ 95. I give practical advice to help others through complicated situations.
_____ 96. I enjoy learning about how organizations function.
_____ 97. I enjoy pioneering new undertakings.
_____ 98. I am good at and enjoy working with my hands.
_____ 99. I am creative and imaginative.
_____ 100. I can identify preaching, teaching, or communication that is not true to the Bible.
_____ 101. I like motivating others to take steps for spiritual growth.
_____ 102. I openly and confidently tell others what Christ has done for me.
_____ 103. I regularly challenge others to trust God.
_____ 104. I give generously due to my commitment to stewardship.

3 = Consistently, 2 = Most of the time, 1 = Some of the time, 0 = Not at all

_____ 105. I feel comfortable being a helper, assisting others to do their job more effectively.

_____ 106. I do whatever I can to make people feel that they belong.

_____ 107. I am honored when someone asks me to pray for them.

_____ 108. I discover important Biblical truths when reading or studying Scripture that benefit others in the Body of Christ.

_____ 109. I can cast a vision that others want to be a part of.

_____ 110. I enjoy bringing hope and joy to people living in difficult circumstances.

_____ 111. I will speak God's truth, even in places where it is unpopular or difficult for others to accept.

_____ 112. I can gently restore wandering believers to faith and fellowship.

_____ 113. I can present information and skills to others at a level that makes it easy for them to grasp and apply to their lives.

_____ 114. I can apply Scriptural truth that others regard as practical and helpful.

_____ 115. I can visualize a coming event, anticipate potential problems, and develop backup plans.

_____ 116. I am able to orchestrate or oversee several church ministries.

_____ 117. I am able to design and construct things that help the church.

_____ 118. I regularly need to get alone to reflect and develop my imagination.

_____ 119. I can sense when demonic forces are at work in a person or situation.

_____ 120. I am able to challenge or rebuke others in order to foster spiritual growth.

_____ 121. I seek opportunities to talk about spiritual matters with unbelievers.

_____ 122. I can move forward in spite of position or lack of support when I sense God's blessing on an undertaking.

---

3 = Consistently, 2 = Most of the time, 1 = Some of the time, 0 = Not at all

_____ 123. I believe I have been given an abundance of resources so that I may give more to the Lord's work.

_____ 124. I readily and happily use my natural or learned skills to help wherever needed.

_____ 125. I can make people feel at ease even in unfamiliar surroundings.

_____ 126. I often see specific results in direct response to my prayers.

_____ 127. I confidently share my knowledge and insights with others.

_____ 128. I figure out where we need to go and help others to get there.

_____ 129. I enjoy doing practical things for others who are in need.

_____ 130. I feel compelled to expose sin wherever I see it and to challenge people to repentance.

_____ 131. I enjoy patiently but firmly nurturing others in their development as believers.

_____ 132. I enjoy explaining things to people so that they can grow spiritually and personally.

_____ 133. I have insights into how to solve problems that others do not see.

---

3 = Consistently, 2 = Most of the time, 1 = Some of the time, 0 = Not at all

Spiritual Gifts Answer Key:

Enter your scores from the questions above and enter the total of each row. Your highest scores indicate your areas of greatest spiritual gifting.

1 =	20 =	39 =	58 =	77 =	96 =	115 =	T =	A
2 =	21 =	40 =	59 =	78 =	97 =	116 =	T =	B
3 =	22 =	41 =	60 =	79 =	98 =	117 =	T =	C
4 =	23 =	42 =	61 =	80 =	99 =	118 =	T =	D
5 =	24 =	43 =	62 =	81 =	100 =	119 =	T =	E
6 =	25 =	44 =	63 =	82 =	101 =	120 =	T =	F
7 =	26 =	45 =	64 =	83 =	102 =	121 =	T =	G
8 =	27 =	46 =	65 =	84 =	103 =	122 =	T =	H
9 =	28 =	47 =	66 =	85 =	104 =	123 =	T =	I
10 =	29 =	48 =	67 =	86 =	105 =	124 =	T =	J
11 =	30 =	49 =	68 =	87 =	106 =	125 =	T =	K
12 =	31 =	50 =	69 =	88 =	107 =	126 =	T =	L
13 =	32 =	51 =	70 =	89 =	108 =	127 =	T =	M
14 =	33 =	52 =	71 =	90 =	109 =	128 =	T =	N
15 =	34 =	53 =	72 =	91 =	110 =	129 =	T =	O
16 =	35 =	54 =	73 =	92 =	111 =	130 =	T =	P
17 =	36 =	55 =	74 =	93 =	112 =	131 =	T =	Q
18 =	37 =	56 =	75 =	94 =	113 =	132 =	T =	R
19 =	38 =	57 =	76 =	95 =	114 =	133 =	T =	S

Spiritual Gifts Assessment Key:

A = Administration	K = Hospitality
B = Apostleship / Missions	L = Intercession
C = Craftsmanship	M = Knowledge
D = Creative Communication	N = Leadership
E = Discernment	O = Mercy
F = Encouragement	P = Prophecy
G = Evangelism	Q = Shepherding / Pastoring
H = Faith	R = Teaching
I = Giving	S = Wisdom
J = Helps / Service	

SECTION FOUR

DISCOVERING YOUR PLACE

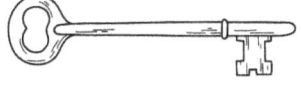

"We have different gifts, according to the grace given to each of us. If your gift is prophesying, then prophesy in accordance with your faith; if it is serving, then serve; if it is teaching, then teach; if it is to encourage, then give encouragement; if it is giving, then give generously; if it is to lead, do it diligently; if it is to show mercy, do it cheerfully."

Romans 12:6-8

4 – Discovering Your Place

Heart Assessment

"Delight yourself in the LORD and he will give you the desires of your heart."
Psalms 37:4

Another way to think of your heart is to think about passion! Take a moment to think about these questions:

What drives you?
- What would you do for God if you knew you couldn't fail?

_____
_____

- What pushes you to action?

_____
_____

- What moves you so deeply that it keeps you awake at night?

_____
_____

Who are the people you most want to help?
- Who do you feel you can influence the most?

_____
_____

- Is there an age range you feel most drawn to? If so, what age group?

_____
_____

- Is there an affinity group you feel most drawn to?

_____

_____

What are the needs you feel most drawn to?
- What are the top two needs you love to meet for people?

_____

_____

- Why do you love meeting those needs?

_____

_____

What cause are you most passionate about?
- What cause or issue makes your heart race?

_____

_____

- Where could you make the greatest impact for God?

_____

_____

Passions - People

Directions: Please check each box that you feel applies to you. The people I would like to serve most are:

- ☐ Children
- ☐ College
- ☐ Disabled
- ☐ Divorced
- ☐ Elderly
- ☐ Empty Nesters
- ☐ Homeless
- ☐ Hospitalized
- ☐ Infants
- ☐ Parents
- ☐ Poor
- ☐ Prisoners
- ☐ Single Parents
- ☐ Singles
- ☐ Teen Moms
- ☐ Unemployed
- ☐ Widowed
- ☐ Women
- ☐ Young Married
- ☐ Youth
- ☐ Other_____
- ☐ Other_____

Passions - Issues and Causes

The issues or causes that I feel most strongly about are:

- ☐ Abortion
- ☐ Abuse/Violence
- ☐ Addictions
- ☐ At-Risk Children
- ☐ Child Care
- ☐ Compulsive Behavior
- ☐ Deafness
- ☐ Discipleship
- ☐ Economics
- ☐ Education
- ☐ Environment
- ☐ Ethics
- ☐ Family
- ☐ Finances
- ☐ Health/Fitness
- ☐ HIV/AIDS
- ☐ Human Trafficking
- ☐ Law/Justice System
- ☐ Literacy
- ☐ Marriage/Family
- ☐ Parenting
- ☐ Politics
- ☐ Poverty
- ☐ Sanctity of Life
- ☐ Spiritual Apathy
- ☐ Violence
- ☐ Other_____

Put the top 3 to 6 People and Issues and Causes on the S.H.A.P.E. Results Profile on page 115.

Abilities Assessment

Each of us has abilities that we have discovered and learned over our lifetime. Read through this list of specialized abilities and check the abilities that you excel at and love doing.

Professional
- ☐ Advertising
- ☐ Career Counseling
- ☐ Carpet Cleaning
- ☐ Chiropractic
- ☐ Computer Programming
- ☐ Counseling
- ☐ Day Care Director
- ☐ Dental
- ☐ Engineer
- ☐ Financial
- ☐ Journalist/Writer
- ☐ Landscaping
- ☐ Law Enforcement
- ☐ Legal
- ☐ Medical
- ☐ Mental Health
- ☐ Paramedic/EMT
- ☐ Personnel Manager
- ☐ Public Relations
- ☐ Radio
- ☐ Social Work
- ☐ Systems analyst
- ☐ Television
- ☐ Window Washing

Music
- ☐ Arranger
- ☐ Bassist
- ☐ Chart Songs
- ☐ Choir
- ☐ Choir Director
- ☐ Composer
- ☐ Drummer
- ☐ Guitar player
- ☐ Keyboard player
- ☐ Other Instruments
- ☐ Vocalist

Art
- ☐ Artist
- ☐ Crafts
- ☐ Decorating
- ☐ Graphic Design
- ☐ Multimedia
- ☐ Photography

Leader
- ☐ Couples
- ☐ Elementary
- ☐ Junior High
- ☐ Men's Group
- ☐ Preschool
- ☐ Senior High
- ☐ Singles
- ☐ Tutoring
- ☐ Women's Group

Machinist
- ☐ Auto Mechanic
- ☐ Computer Repair
- ☐ Copier Repair
- ☐ Diesel Mechanic
- ☐ Mechanics
- ☐ Small Engine

Missions
- ☐ Evangelism
- ☐ Missionary

Drama
- ☐ Acting
- ☐ Dance
- ☐ Mime/Clown
- ☐ Poet
- ☐ Writer

Production
- ☐ Lighting
- ☐ Producer
- ☐ Set Design
- ☐ Sound
- ☐ Stagehand
- ☐ Studio Recording
- ☐ Video

Construction
- ☐ Architect
- ☐ Cabinets
- ☐ Carpenter
- ☐ Carpet
- ☐ Concrete
- ☐ Drafting
- ☐ Drywall
- ☐ Electrical
- ☐ Finishing
- ☐ General Contractor
- ☐ Heating/AC
- ☐ Interior Design
- ☐ Masonry
- ☐ Painting
- ☐ Papering
- ☐ Plumbing
- ☐ Roofing
- ☐ Telephones
- ☐ Tile

General
- ☐ Bookstore
- ☐ Cashier
- ☐ Child Care
- ☐ Customer Service
- ☐ Food Service
- ☐ Tax Deductions
- ☐ Transportation
- ☐ Weddings

Maintenance
- ☐ Building
- ☐ Cleaning
- ☐ Gardening
- ☐ Grounds

Sports
- ☐ Basketball
- ☐ Football
- ☐ General Athlete
- ☐ Golf
- ☐ Lifeguard
- ☐ Soccer
- ☐ Softball
- ☐ Tennis

Personality Assessment

Understanding the personality God has given you will help you more effectively express your spiritual gifts, heart, and abilities for HIS sake.

"Like stained glass, our different personalities Reflect God's light in many colors and patterns."
--Rick Warren

We are going to focus on only two aspects of your personality:
How you are **Energized** and how you are **Organized**.

Directions:

- For each statement, circle the number towards the statement that most accurately describes what you would prefer in most situations.
- Do not answer according to what you feel is expected by a spouse, family member, employer, etc.
- Select the behavior or perspective that would come naturally to you if you knew there were NO restrictions or consequences for your personal expression.

How are you Energized?

I'm more comfortable:
| Doing things for people | 1 | 2 | 3 | 4 | Being with people |

When doing a task, I tend to:
| Focus on the goal | 1 | 2 | 3 | 4 | Focus on relationships |

I get more excited about:
| Advancing a cause | 1 | 2 | 3 | 4 | Creating community |

I feel I've accomplished something when I've:
| Gotten a job done | 1 | 2 | 3 | 4 | Built a relationship |

It is more important to start a meeting:
| On time | 1 | 2 | 3 | 4 | When everyone gets there |

I'm more concerned with:
| Meeting a deadline | 1 | 2 | 3 | 4 | Maintaining the team |

I place higher value on:
Action   1   2   3   4   Communication

Add all the numbers you circled and record the total here. Total:_____

If your score was 7-17: You are more task oriented.
If your total was 18-28: You are more people oriented.

How are You Organized?

While on vacation I prefer to:
Be spontaneous   1   2   3   4   Follow a set plan

I prefer to set guidelines that are:
General   1   2   3   4   Specific

I prefer projects that have:
Variety   1   2   3   4   Routine

I like to:
Play it by ear   1   2   3   4   Stick to a plan

I find routine:
Boring   1   2   3   4   Restful

I accomplish tasks best:
By working it out as I go   1   2   3   4   By following a plan

Add all the numbers you circled and record the total here. Total:_____

If your score was 7-17: You are unstructured.
If your total was 18-28: You are structured.

Record your results below for your record and on the S.H.A.P.E. Profile Results on page 115.

I am _____/_____.
        Task or **People**   **Structured** or **Unstructured**

Experience Assessment

"Praise be to the God and Father of our Lord Jesus Christ, the Father of compassion and the God of all comfort, who comforts us in all our troubles, so that we can comfort those in any trouble with the comfort we ourselves have received from God."   2 Corinthians 1:3-4

Take a moment to think about these different experiences and how they have impacted your life:

- Educational experiences – favorite subjects in school, special training, etc
- Ministry experience – how you've served in the past
- Painful experiences – problems, hurts, trials, etc
- Spiritual experiences – meaningful decisions, special times with God, times you felt especially close to God

1. What educational experiences have you had?

    _____
    _____
    _____
    _____
    _____
    _____

2. What ministry experiences have you had?

    _____
    _____
    _____
    _____
    _____
    _____

3. What painful experiences have you had?

   _____
   _____
   _____
   _____
   _____
   _____

4. What spiritual experiences have you had?

   _____
   _____
   _____
   _____
   _____
   _____

S.H.A.P.E. Profile Results

Spiritual Gifts
List your top 1-4 Gifts/Gift Mix (If you have ties, pick the one that you feel fits best.)
FROM PAGES 94-102

1._____ 3._____

2. _____ 4. _____

Heart
List your top 3-6 themes, people groups, issues and/or causes that you feel most strongly about:
FROM PAGES 105-108

1._____ 4._____

2. _____ 5. _____

3. _____ 6. _____

Abilities
List your top 3-6 themes, people groups, issues and/or causes that you feel most strongly about:
FROM PAGES 109-110

1._____ 4._____

2. _____ 5. _____

3. _____ 6. _____

Personality
Circle below:
I am Task-Oriented or People-Oriented / I am Structured or Unstructured

Experience
Highlight your Spiritual, Painful, Educational & Ministry Experience:

_____

_____

_____

SECTION FIVE

EXPLORING FURTHER HELP

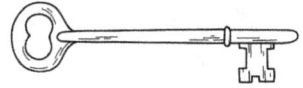

"So then, just as you received Christ Jesus as Lord, continue to live in him, rooted and built up in him, strengthened in the faith as you were taught, and overflowing with thankfulness."
Colossians 2:6-7

5 – Exploring Further Help

Congratulations! You've completed the workbook! Throughout this workbook, you have learned how to connect with God by reading the Bible, praying, and spending time with God. You have also worked through your own healing journey by learning to forgive others, breaking soul ties, and taking care of yourself. Lastly, you learned the importance of serving others and discovered your giftings and place of service.

I hope you found this workbook beneficial, healing, and empowering. If you find that you still need help discovering your identity, healing from the past, or finding your purpose, I would be happy to guide you along your journey. There are many other strategies and tools we can use to help you grow and heal.

I pray that God would touch the places of your heart that you never thought could be healed and that growth would take deep root in your life. I pray that God would help you in all areas of your life and that you would see life as a true blessing. I pray God would help you rise up to become the person He has called you to be and that you would step into the power and authority He has given you. In Jesus' name, Amen!

If you would like to do further counseling, please send an email to info@daretolivefree.net with your results page from the S.H.A.P.E. Assessment attached. Also, in the body of the email, please give a short explanation of the areas where you need help. I will get back to you as soon as possible with availability.

Thanks for completing this workbook! I hope and pray it was exactly what you needed.

Love & Prayers,
Rachel Dick
918-800-1252
www.daretolivefree.net

www.ingramcontent.com/pod-product-compliance
Lightning Source LLC
Chambersburg PA
CBHW080913170426
43201CB00017B/2309